RĪGA

JOURNEY THROUGH THE CENTURIES

CONTENTS

Layout and design artist: Andris Lamsters
Photographer: Leons Balodis
Accompanying text: Māra Siliņa
Computer design: Oskars Stalidzāns
Editor-in-chief: Skaidrīte Naumova
Additional photographs from museum archives.

UDK 770 (474.3)(084)
Ri 481
ISBN 9984-592-77-4

Printed in «Preses Nams»,
Riga, Latvia

Riga is a beautiful city, Rigans proudly state. Visitors also sing Riga's praises, calling it one of the most beautiful and interesting cities in all of Europe. With its striking skyline of church steeples mirrored in the Daugava River, Riga has graced the canvases of numerous artists.

Riga's buildings reflect almost every Western European architectural style and historic period. Besides the Romanesque and Gothic style, Mannerism, Baroque, Classical and particularly Art Nouveau are all a part of Rigas architectural panorama. A stroll through Riga's streets bears witness to its 800 year history.

Riga's name was first mentioned in 1198, but its official founding date is 1201, when Bishop Albert relocated his residence from nearby Ikšķile to a spot on the banks of the ancient Riga River, where already in the 11th and 12th century the Livs and ancient Latvians had established settlements. The name of the city derived from the Riga or Ridzene River, that flowed into the Daugava River. The mouth of the Daugava was a profitable port location, which eventually attracted German traders, who were searching for new transit routes to the East, and the Crusade, which was searching for new peoples to subjugate.

Medieval Riga grew and developed rapidly into a major port city. As a member of the Hanseatic League, Riga played an important role in trade between the East and the West. After the collapse of the Livonian Order, Riga was subsequently ruled by Polish, Russian and Swedish forces. Through the years, it remained an economic, cultural and political center for the Baltic region.

On November 18, 1918, the independent Republic of Latvia was proclaimed with Riga as its capital city. On August 21, 1991, following 50 years of Soviet occupation, Latvia regained its independent status, with its capital Riga now totaling almost one million inhabitants.

DOM CHURCH

The **Dom Church**, the cathedral of the
Archbishop of the Latvian Lutheran Evangelical
Church, is a superb architectural and artistic
landmark of the 13th–20th centuries. Bishop Albert
blessed the first stone laid in 211. The church, in
homage to the Virgin Mary, was built simultaneously
with a monastery. Both were connected with a
crosswalk on the buildings southern side, creating an
inner courtyard. The bishops castle was also a part of
the enormous edifice. Following the Reformation,
the Dome complex was taken over by the city. The
Dome School (est.1211), under the auspices of the
monastery, became one of the first non-parochial
schools of higher learning. One of the monasteries
wings housed the city library.

The church's oldest sections are examples of the Romanesque style. Gothic-style additions. A vaulted 118 meter walkway, whose ancient arches are enclosed in an inner courtyard, is one of the most superb examples of Medieval architecture in the Baltics.

The church's main portal, completed in the 13th century, is to one side of the building, on the northern facade. The portal at its western end was constructed in 1862, along with the main entrance.

The many multi-colored stained-glass windows add radiance to the interior. They were prepared at the end of the 19th and beginning of the 20th century by workshops in Riga, Munich and Dresden. The altar was designed in 1896, renovated in 1989. The intricately designed wood pulpit was prepared in 1641, but the angel was placed above the pulpit in 1817.

The renowned church organ was completed by the Ludwigsburg (Germany) company Walcker and Co in 1884. With its 124 pitches, 6718 wood and metal pipes, the organ was the largest and most modern instrument of its day. Its vividly detailed engraved wood facade decorates the organ, designed from 16th–18th century.

Bottom left: Coat of Arms of Blackheads Association, 1694.
Page 9, bottom left: Epitaph for Nikolaus von Himsel, 1764.

Dom Square was created in the 1860s–1890s when the Medieval structure was razed, clearing the view of the church's western portal. The square received its current appearance in 1936 when buildings were torn down on the northern and northwestern sides of the church. Ornate Eclectic and Art Nouveau style buildings were constructed opposite the church in the 19th and 20th centuries.

Near the church's entrance is **Herder Square**, that features a statue dedicated to the renowned German writer, philosopher and enlightener Johann Gottfried Herder (1744–1803). From 1764 to 1771, Herder was a teacher and parson at the Dom School. He collected and popularized the folk songs of many nations and was the very first to collect and translate Latvia folk songs – the dainas.

Top: Herder Monument.
Bottom: Allegorical figure in the Riga Stock Exchange's facade.

CITY FORTIFICATION

With its typical fortification system consisting of ramparts and towers, Riga was no exception to the rule in Medieval cities. By 1330, Riga boasted as many as 28 towers with the **Powder Tower** (Pulvertornis) the most prominent among them because it guarded the main land entrance to the city. Its original name, the Sand Tower (Smilšu tornis) derived from the sand mounds located outside the fortress walls and the Sand Road, that led into the city. The tower was destroyed in 1621, when Swedish forces, led by King Gustav II Adolph, attacked Riga. It was rebuilt in the same century. The tower stored gunpowder, hence its name. Today, the tower is adjacent to the Latvian War Museum.

Above left: The Swedish Gate, Trokšņu Street.
Below: The fortress wall with the Rāmera Tower and Jacobs Barracks on Torņa Street.

Page 12
Bottom right: Portion of the fortification wall at Trokšņu Street, restored in 1987.

The Swedish Gate was constructed in 1698. The gate connected Torņa Street with Trokšņu (Noise) Street, creating a passageway. Trokšņu Street was initially an underdeveloped area, where city citizens gathered inside the wall when alarms were sounded, hence its name, Trokšņu or its earlier name, Trauksmes (alarm) Street.

RIGA CASTLE

The first foundation for the Livonian Order's first castle were laid at the banks of the Daugava River in 1330. It was destroyed in the 15th century following a conflict between the order and the city. A new castle was completed in 1515. Renovations and additions to the edifice came when it was the residence of the Vidzeme governor. During Latvia's first period of independence, the castle served as the presidential palace and does to this day.

ST. JACOB'S CHURCH

St. Jacob's Church, the cathedral of the Roman Catholic archbishop. The church was first mentioned in chronicles in 1225. It was constructed outside the Riga fortification wall and was meant to serve parishioners from outlying areas. Its early history is rather complicated. At one time it was utilized by Cistercian nuns. During the Reformation, St.Jacob's was the first church to hail the new religious movement and subsequently held the first Lutheran services. The church has also been the home for the Jesuit Order and a Swedish garrison. Its tall, slender spire is one of the vertical accents in Riga's skyline.

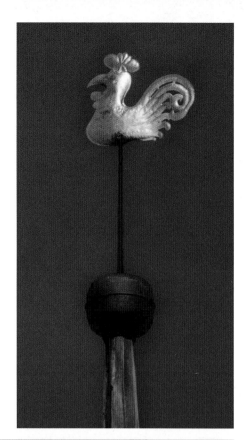

The Riga Royal Lyceum (also called the Karl Lyceum) was founded in 1675. The famed Baltic ethnographer Johann Christoph Brotze (1742-1823) worked here as a teacher for 46 years.

Medieval dwellings on Mazā Pils Street

At right, the oldest brick house in Riga, constructed in the late 15th century. The corner of the house, with its tall pediment faces the street. A craftsman and his family lived and worked on the first floor. Completed articles and raw materials were stored in the basement and attic.

At left: Portal, St. Jacob's Church.

Doorside stones adorned with various emblems, seals and figural compositions at both ends, graced the entranceway.

Top right: Portal, Jēkaba Street.

ST. JOHN'S CHURCH

St. John's Church dates back to 1297. Originally a small Dominican cloister chapel, the church was destroyed in the 15th century. It was rebuilt at the end of the 15th century in the Gothic style. The church's west end features a gradated pediment – the most imposing of its kind in Riga, while the interior boasts a magnificent webbed vaulted ceiling. The church was enlarged in the 16th century in the Mannerism style.

Top left: Baroque altar, St. John's Church.
Top right: Interior, St. John's Church.
Below: Skārņu Street. First building from left – St. George's Church.

St. George's Church is the oldest brick edifice in Riga (13th century). It was built as a chapel of the Knights of the Order of the Brothers of the Sword. After serving as a place of worship, it was utilized as a warehouse. The building is now the home of the Museum of Applied Arts.

Konventhof (Convent Courtyard) is the former courtyard of the order's castle. In the 14th century, the Holy Ghost Convent was transferred to the territory of the former castle. The buildings were reconstructed through the years but have retained their Holy Ghost symbol – the pigeon.

Mentzendorff House. Built in 1695 and reconstructed on many occasions over the years. A branch of the Museum of the History of Riga and Navigation opened here in 1991. The interior features striking ceiling and wall paintings.

The Blackheads House, initially called the New House, was built in 1334 in Town Square, Old Riga. In the 17th century its sole owners were the *Blackheads Compagnie* – a society of bold and single merchants. In World War II the building was turned to ruins. It was

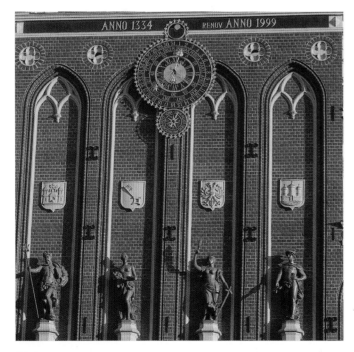

reconstructed in 1999. The House is a perfect venue for festive occasions, conferences, public gatherings and parties. The ancient basement of the House accomodates the exhibition "From the History of the Blackheads House". Viewing the pictures and sculptures one can follow through the numerous reconstructions of the House, starting with 1522 when the doorside stones with figures of Madonna and St. Mauritius were placed at the entrance door. In the late 19th century the House was decorated with coats of arms of Hansa towns and allegoric sculptures of Neptune, Mercury, Unity and Peace. In the anteroom of the basement there is a dedication to the restorers of the Blackheads House who had fulfilled the ancient message above the entrance: "Should I ever perish, then Come and put me up again."

Mārstaļu Street. The merchant Reutern elaborate house was built in the Baroque style. Attention is drawn to the nearby Reformed Church, with its Baroque gable and graceful steeple.

St. John's Courtyard. Located on the former territory of the Bishop's castle, later a Dominican monastery, St. John's Courtyard features a portion of the Riga fortification wall.

Top: The Blackheads House.
Bottom: Detail, facade of the Blackheads House.

Page 25
Top left: Entrance to St. John's Courtyard.
Top right: Mārstaļu Street. Bottom: St. John's Courtyard.

ST. PETER'S CHURCH

St. Peter's Church is the tallest building in Old Town Riga. First mentioned in chronicles in 1209 as a merchants or city church, this brick house of worship, however, appears to have been built in the second half of the 13th century, but extensively renovated in the 14th–15th century.

Lower left: St. Peter's Church's Gothic portal in the altar's north wall.
Lower right: West facade Baroque side portal.

The church's eastern end features a semicircular passage with a characteristic Gothic chapel wreath, while the interior featured ornate cross and stellar vaults. Its current appearance stands from the 17th century when its west facade was redone with three elaborate entrance portals with Baroque sculptures. In 1690, builder R.Bindenschu's design served as a basis for the 64.5 meter steeple, which was the tallest such wooden structure in all of Europe in its day. The steeple has fallen victim to fire on several occasions, the last time in 1941, when World War II reached Riga. Reconstruction of a metal steeple began in 1968 and was unveiled in 1973, towering 120 meters over Old Town Riga.

Top left: Stained glass window in the vestry.
Top center: St. Peter's former steeple-top rooster.
Bottom left: Blue Guard tomb.
Bottom right: Epitaph.

Page 30
Interior, St. Peter's Church.

When the new fortification plan for Riga was created in the 17th century with its ramparts, moats, bastions, and ravelins, the antiquated defense wall was razed. In some locations, it remained as a part of the new street layout. As the city grew in size, more buildings rose outside the former wall.

After the fortification wall was torn down, in the period 1857–1863, one of the most beautiful Riga ensembles was created, the so-called **Boulevard Circle** with its canal-lined trees and shrubs. Eclectic and Art Nouveau are the prevalent architectural styles in this area.

Top: Aspazijas Boulevard
Bottom: Old Town's Cat House was named after its many charming cat sculptures.

Page 32
Above: Hotel de Rome, Aspazijas Boulevard.
Below: Buildings adjoining former fortification wall.

Canal greenery.

The National Opera House.

The Freedom Monument
(Sculptor K.Zāle, architect E.Stālbergs, constructed 1931–1935)
The Freedom Monument – the conscience of the Latvian people, symbol of its spiritual strength and the ideal of freedom. The 42 meter tall monument's main motif is the inscription, "For Fatherland and Freedom" and it was built with donations made by Latvian citizens. A multi-leveled structure, an obelisk rises from a series of figural compositions. The symbol of freedom – a woman standing atop the obelisk, holding three stars raised high above her head. They symbolize Latvias three historic regions – Kurzeme, Vidzeme, Latgale.

Top: Mother Latvia
Bottom left: Lāčplēsis, the Bear Slayer.
Bottom right, Sculptural figures, Labor.

The music center Vernisāža opened its doors in 1998 in **Vērmanes Garden Park**. The park, opened in 1817, is named after its benefactress, the Big Guild chairmans widow, Anna Gertrude Wöhrmann. Through the years, it has become one of the most popular recreation areas in Riga.

Riga parks, gardens and landscaping feature sculptures, fountains and monuments to prominent writers and artists.

Top right: Monument to poet Jānis Rainis (1865-1929) on the Esplanade.
Bottom left: Monument honoring writer Rūdolfs Blaumanis (1863-1908), Canal greenery.
Page 38
Lower right: Monument to artist Kārlis Padegs (1911-1940), Vērmanes Garden Park.

At the end of the 19th century and the beginning of the 20th century, several important public buildings in the Eclectic and Art Nouveau style were constructed in and around the new **Boulevard Circle**.

Riga City Council (the former Mortgage Society Bank), designed in the Neoclassical style.

The National Theater, originally the (Russian) Second City Theater combines Neobaroque, Neoclassical and Art Nouveau features. The Latvian republic was proclaimed here on November 18, 1918.

Academy of Art
The former Stock Exchange Business School building, its architecture consists of Gothic brick and Art Nouveau features.

Russian Orthodox Cathedral
A distinct Byzantine influence is noted in its forms.

State Museum of Art
An imposing edifice with grand Neobaroque characteristics.

ART NOUVEAU

Over the years, Riga has gained a reputation as an Art Nouveau metropolis with over one-third of its buildings designed in this style. Riga's Art Nouveau architecture reflects influences from Germany, Austria and Finland. Along with the decorative Eclectic manner, a Nationalistic strain is also seen which tones down the ostentatiousness. The historic Romantic and perpendicular Art Nouveau are also extensively represented in Riga, as is the National Romantic design.

Many Riga buildings are designed by M.Eisenstein, reflecting an affinity for Ectectic-Art Nouveau.

Below: Rental property at Alberta Street 4.
Architect: M.Eisenstein, 1904
Top left: Decorative element, Alberta Street 6.
Top right: Facade detail, Alberta Street 2a.

Strēlnieku Street 4a. A former private school, now home of the Stockholm School of Economics. The facade features rich ornamental and sculptural motifs.

Rental property at Alberta Street 12 was built with Rationalistic Art Nouveau forms with various stylized Romantic details, close to the National Romantic style. Inside – a memorial apartment-museum, where the illustrious Latvian artist Janis Rozentāls and writer Rūdolfs Blaumanis once lived.
Architect K.Pēkšēns, 1903.

Rental property with shops at Brīvības 55 is one of the first Art Nouveau buildings in the former environs of Riga. The facade is designed with distinct Romantic touches.
Architect: V.Neimanis, 1900.

Top left: Detail, building facade on Elizabetes Street.
Top right: Detail, facade on Smilšu Street
Below: Alberta Street 12.

Page 47
Top: Detail, building facade at Elizabetes Street 10b.
Below: Brīvības Street 55.

Rental property with shops at Kronvalda Boulevard 10 represents the National Romantic style. Various natural materials grace the facade. Ethnographic motifs are featured in the ornamental reliefs.
Architects: K.Pēkšēns and E.Laube, 1907.

Above: Detail, facade at Alberta Street 11.
Below: Portal, Kronvalda Boulevard 10.

Atis Ķeniņš School at Tērbatas Street 15/17. One of the first buildings in the National Romantic style in Riga. Architects: K.Pēkšēns and E.Laube, 1905.

Top right: Detail, building at K.Valdemāra Street 20.
Below: Brīvības Street 47.

Page 50: Tērbatas Street 15/17.

Rental property with shops at Brīvības Street 47 constructed in the spirit of National Romanticism, considered one of the most characteristic of all buildings designed by architect E.Laube in this style. The form is based on local (folk) construction methods, but its decorative composition – stylized ethnographic motifs. 1908.

The Riga Latvian Society House. Rebuilt in 1910, (designed by architect E.Pole) after the original building was destroyed by fire. The Riga Latvian Society was founded in 1868. Its goal – the promotion of Latvian nationalistic conscience and the Latvian awareness in every walk of life.

Above: Decorative frieze, façade at the Riga Latvian Society House. Artist: Janis Rozentals (1909-1910), based on Latvian mythology.

MUSEUMS

THE STATE MUSEUM OF ART

The State Museum of Art's Latvian fine arts collection encompasses the period from the mid-18th century up to 1945. The museum also includes the largest collection of Russian art in the Baltic states (16th to 20th century) and an impressive collection of Balto-Germanic art.

The large edifice was built in 1903–1905 to specifically house the Riga City Art Museum and the Art Advancement Society.

The permanent collection is displayed on two floors. The first floor covers Baltic and Russian masterpieces from the 18th and 19th century, including the works of Nicholas Roerich.

The second floor houses a chronological overview of the development of Latvian art from the mid-19th century to 1945.

The album contains the artwork of early 20th century Latvian masters.

Page 53
Top: V. Purvitis. "Springtime Waters". 1910.
Bottom: J.Rozentals. "Joyful Children". 1901.
Photo: M.Brašmane & A. Toše.

Top left: J.Grosvalds.
"Baghdad Market".
1918–1919.
Top right: J.Kazaks.
"Refugees". 1917.
Center: N.Strunke.
"Self-Portrait With Doll".
Early 20th century.
Bottom left: L.Svemps.
"Still Life With Old
Dishes". 1922.
Bottom right: V.Tone.
"At The Window". 1932.

Photo:
M.Brašmane.

Top left: G.Eliass.
"Woman In A Bar With
A Fan". 1910s.
Top right: K.Ubāns.
"Last Snowfall". 1937.
Center left: J.Tīdemanis.
"In Port". "The First
Glove". 1930s.
Center right: K.Miesnieks.
"Daily Bread". 1929.
Bottom left: K.Padegs.
"Buy White Roses". 1935.
Bottom right: G.Klucis.
"Dynamic City". 1919.

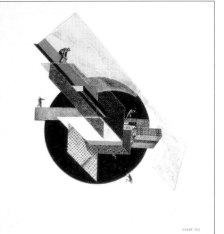

THE LATVIAN MUSEUM OF FOREIGN ART

With works from the private collections of N. von Himsel, D. De Robiani, and others, in 1773 the museum became one of the richest repositories of foreign artwork in Latvia. On view are works from Ancient Egypt and Greece, Rome, the Far East and India. The permanent collection contains Western European art from the 15th century to today. Italian painting is represented by the masters of the 17th and 18th century. The museum features paintings from the Netherlands as far back as the 16th century, but the works of Dutch painters from the 17th and 18th century are the pride of the museum. The largest collection is that of paintings by German artists from the 16th–17th century. Another notable acquisition is a series of paintings by Belgian artists, presented to the museum by the artists and their families. The graphic art collection contains over 9,000 works created in various techniques, with drawings by Rembrandt, Ostade, Kahlo and Goya among them. The sculpture collection contains about 150 original works as well as several hundred medals and plaques. In cooperation with the Meissen China Manufacturer, the museum has also added contemporary China to its collection.

Top: P.Aertsen, the Elder (1540-1603) "Christ on the Cross". The Netherlands.
Bottom: Unknown. "Prodigal Son". Germany. 16th century.

Page 57
Top left: J.Massys (1510-1575). "St. Hieronymus".
Top right: H.J. van der Lamen (1606-1659). "Prodigal Son". Flanders.
Center left: M.de Hondecoeter (1636-1695). "Cockfight". The Netherlands.

Photo: G.Kajons & A.Toše.

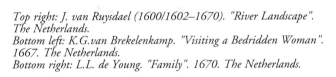

Top right: J. van Ruysdael (1600/1602–1670). "River Landscape".
The Netherlands.
Bottom left: K.G.van Brekelenkamp. "Visiting a Bedridden Woman".
1667. The Netherlands.
Bottom right: L.L. de Young. "Family". 1670. The Netherlands.

Center left: German porcelain. Vase with Snow Balls. Meissen, Germany. 1756, 1763.
Bottom left: E.H. Landshire. "Rest". 1839. England.
Bottom right: L.G.E. Isabey. "The Fishermen's Girl". 1850. France.

Top left: Tiber Banks Near Aqua Achetoza". 1835. Germany.
Top right: K. Spitzweg (1808-1885). "The Loner". Germany.

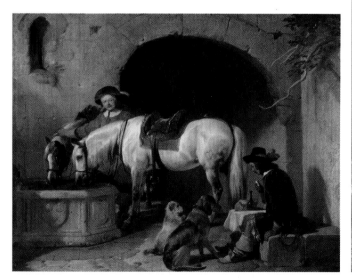

THE MUSEUM OF THE HISTORY OF RIGA AND NAVIGATION

The Riga Dome Church complex in Old Town Riga houses one of the first museums in Europe and the oldest in the Baltic region – the Museum of History of Riga and Navigation, founded in 1773. Like many other museums in Riga, its basis was the private collection of noted Riga physician Nikolaus von Himsel, which he donated to the city.

In over two decades, the museum has become one of the largest and most important treasury of Riga's history with over 500,000 items included in its repository.

An inscription (in Latin) adorns the building's entrance: "With the help of God, future descendants, sincerely honoring the memory of their forebearers, bequeth the newly renovated former cathedral monastery for the arts and sciences. In the year of our Lord, 1899."

Top left: The museum building.
Top right: Vestibule stairwell.
Moors from the former House of
Blackheads greet visitors.
Center left: Riga physician Nicholas
von Himmsel (1729–1764).
Bottom right: Riga minting tools and
coins, 15th century.

Photo: I.Gradovskis.

City life in the Middle Ages was primarily led by the activities of various associations and societies. The main such organizations in Riga were the Big or St. Mary's Guild, which united Riga's merchants, and the Small or St. John's Guild, which consisted of craftsmen, and the Blackheads' Society, whose members were unwed foreign merchants.

Top left: Bishop Albert's seal, 13th century.
Top right: The Death of St. Mary. The Large Guild's altar. Wood carving. 15th–16th century.
Center: Ornamentation for a ship's rudder. Wood. 17th century.
Center right: Cup-statuette "Swedish King Gustav II Adolph". Silver. Augsburg, Germany.
D. Schwestermueller. Late 17th century. From the Blackheads' collection – one of the largest and most opulent silver collections in the Baltic region.
Top left: St. John The Baptist, the Small Guild's guardian. Wood. Early 16th century.
Top right: Councilmember and burghermeister Alexander Gottschalk Sengbusch. J.G. Sigmund. 1890s.

Photo: I. Gradovskis.

Top left: Chest designed with Riga city seals. Made by A. Naika, designed by A. Dzervitis. 1936.
Top right: Certificate of contribution to the Freedom Monument and medal, "For Outstanding Achievement In Erecting The Freedom Monument".

Latvia's first period of independence is charted in the exhibition, "Riga and Rigans: 1918-1940".

Museum resources also include chronicles of relatively recent events, one of which is (1991) now written in history as the Barricades.

Center left: "Signāli. 1991. I".
Kurts Fridrihsons' sketch from his Barricades series.
Lower left: The Barricades period. Photo: I. Gradovskis.
Lower right: Big Kristaps (St. Christopher). Kristaps' woodcut sculpture was a favorite of Riga inhabitants as far back as the early 16th century. Repaired and restored multiple times over the years. Photo: I. Gradovskis.

LATVIAN MUSEUM OF HISTORY

Founded in 1869, the Latvian Museum of History contains the largest repository of valuable examples of Latvian material culture. The museum contains over 600,000 historical items. The first part of the permanent exposition depicts the arrival of the first nomadic tribes in the territory of present day Latvia and cultural development in the Stone, Bronze and Iron Ages. Items, found in archeological digs over the years, reflect the life of the ancient Livs and Latvians, through their apparel, adornment and jewelry, ironmaking, and various household tools. The theme of the second part of the exposition is ethnographic with Latvian folk costumes, jewelry, farming and fishing tools and household items all on display. Esthetic pleasure can be found in the permanent collection, "Sacred Art", featuring wooden sculptures from the 14th century through the 20th century.

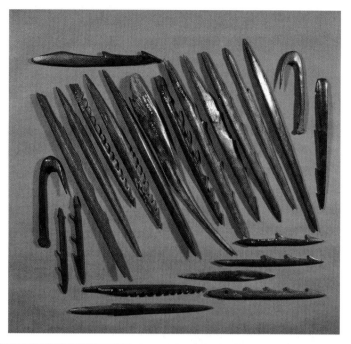